MY WILD LIFE

I am a
monkey!

By Camilla de la Bedoyere

Miles
Kelly

Look out for the 'Ask for help!' boxes. You will need help from an adult to do these activities.

Ask for help!

First published in 2012 by Miles Kelly Publishing Ltd
Harding's Barn, Bardfield End Green, Thaxted, Essex, CM6 3PX, UK
Copyright © Miles Kelly Publishing Ltd 2012

© 2012 Discovery Communications, LLC. Animal Planet and logo are trademarks of Discovery Communications, LLC, used under license. All rights reserved. www.animalplanet.co.uk

10 9 8 7 6 5 4 3 2 1

Publishing Director Belinda Gallagher
Creative Director Jo Cowan
Editorial Director Rosie McGuire
Editor Sarah Parkin
Designers Jo Cowan, Joe Jones
Image Manager Liberty Newton
Production Manager Elizabeth Collins
Reprographics Stephan Davis, Anthony Cambray, Jennifer Hunt

ISBN 978-1-84810-618-5

Printed in China

British Library Cataloguing-in-Publication Data
A catalogue record for this book is available from the British Library

ACKNOWLEDGEMENTS

The publishers would like to thank Mike Foster (Maltings Partnership), Joe Jones, and Richard Watson (Bright Agency) for the illustrations they contributed to this book.

All other artwork from the Miles Kelly Artwork Bank.

The publishers would like to thank the following sources for the use of their photographs:
t = top, b = bottom, l = left, r = right, c = centre, bg = background, rt = repeated throughout

BOOK
Cover (front) Ingo Arndt/Minden Pictures/FLPA; (back, clockwise from tr) gopause/Shutterstock, Mariia Sats/Shutterstock, Anna Kucherova/Shutterstock, Michael Woodruff/Shutterstock
Alamy 6 dbimages
FLPA 4–5 Pete Oxford/Minden Pictures; 7(tl) Ignacio Yufera; 11(t) Ignacio Yufera; 12 Pete Oxford/Minden Pictures; 13(tl) Neil Bowman, (r) Edward Myles; 14–15 Piotr Naskrecki/Minden Pictures; 18 Ingo Arndt/Minden Pictures; 21(r) Paul Hobson
Fotolia Heading panel(rt) Darren Hester
Nature Picture Library 15(br) Andy Rouse; 21(tl) Yukihiro Fukuda
Photo Discs/ImageState 16–17(bg)
Shutterstock Joke panel(rt) Tropinina Olga; Learn a Word panel(rt) donatas1205; 1 Eric Isselée; 2 Envita; 3 Worakit Sirijinda; 5(gorilla) Mike Price, (orang-utan) javarman, (chimpanzee) Stephen Meese; 7(br) Mike Tan C. T.; 8–9(bg) andere; 8(tr) andere, (tl) Jikinaargo, (fruits, also used on page 17) Andra Popovici, (paper, cl) happydancing, (frame, cl) Lisa Fischer, (cr) Anna Ts, (b) jennipenni89, (banana split, b) Melissa Patton; 9(paper, t) House @ Brasil Art Studio, (tl) Noedelhap, (brush stroke, cl) Ambient Ideas; 10 worldswildlifewonders; 11(b) redswept; 16(cr) Mariia Sats, (b) donatas1205; 17(paper, tl) sharpner, (tr) Jana Guothova, (bl) jennipenni89, (cr) Lorelyn Medina; 19(tl) hallam creations, (b) Kjersti Joergensen; 20(b) Eric Gevaert

POSTER
All images are from Shutterstock. (clockwise from tl) defpicture, worldswildlifewonders, Stéphane Bidouze, Dusaleev Viatcheslav, Eric Gevaert, Cynthia Kidwell, Nickolay Stanev

STICKERS
All images are from Shutterstock. (monkey with banana) Mariia Sats, (monkey swinging) andere

Every effort has been made to acknowledge the source and copyright holder of each picture. Miles Kelly Publishing apologizes for any unintentional errors or omissions.

Made with paper from a sustainable forest

www.mileskelly.net
info@mileskelly.net
www.factsforprojects.com

Contents

What are you?

I am a monkey!

I am a type of animal called a primate. Primates are very clever and most have fur.

Humans are primates too!

Furry body

Long arms

Hands with fingers and thumbs

4

Q. Why was the chimp looking sad?

A. He had belly-ape!

What is an ape?

Like monkeys, apes are primates. They are larger than monkeys and don't have tails.

Gorilla

Orang-utan

Chimpanzee

Tail

What do you eat?

We eat lots of different things.

I pick juicy fruits off the trees, but I also like to eat bugs.

Fruit

6

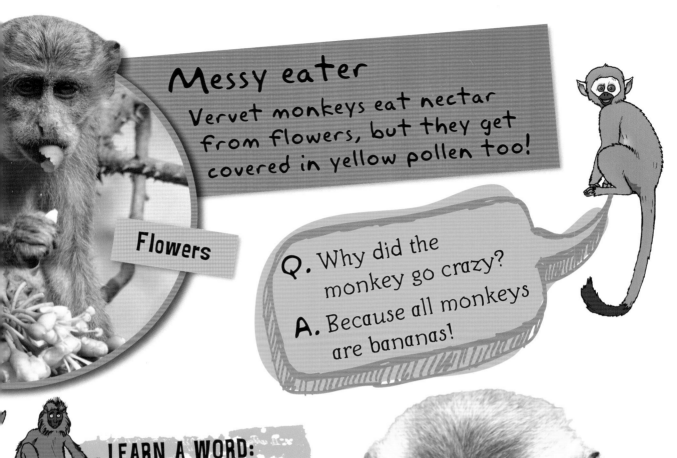

Messy eater

Vervet monkeys eat nectar from flowers, but they get covered in yellow pollen too!

Flowers

Q. Why did the monkey go crazy?

A. Because all monkeys are bananas!

LEARN A WORD:
pollen
Yellow or orange powder found inside flowers.

Leaves

Leaf lolly

Thirsty monkeys lick water off leaves. They tear the leaves before eating them.

Activity time
Get ready to make and do!

Banana split

YOU WILL NEED:
ice cream · banana
whipped cream
cherries

HERE'S HOW: Scoop the
ice cream into a dish.
Then slice the banana
into two long pieces.
Put the banana pieces
on either side of the
ice cream. Decorate
with cream and
cherries. Enjoy!

Go ape!
Ask a grown up to take
you to the park, where
you can practise your
monkey skills safely. You
will need to run, jump,
climb and swing!

Ask for help!

Monkey face

YOU WILL NEED:
paper plate · paints
paintbrush · paper
pencil · scissors · glue

HERE'S HOW:

1. Paint a paper
plate brown, or
glue brown
paper on to it.

2. On separate paper, draw
two eyes, a nose, a mouth
and two ears.

3. Cut them out, and
glue them to
the paper
plate.

Ask for help!

Draw a monkey

Now colour me in and give me a name!

YOU WILL NEED: pencils · paper

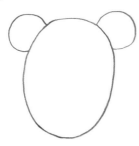

1. Draw a squashed
circle and two
rounded shapes
for ears.

2. Add another
squashed circle
at the bottom.

3. Draw the face
and add two eyes
and a mouth.

Where do you live?

I live in a rainforest, where there are lots of trees.

I can jump and swing from branch to branch. I use my tail to hang from trees.

Spider monkey

LEARN A WORD:
rainforest
Thick forest that grows in warm places where there is both sunshine and rain every day.

Q. Where does a daddy gorilla sit?

A. Anywhere he likes!

Ground life

Gelada baboons live in grassy areas where there are no trees. They sit on the ground and eat grass and roots.

Steam baths

Japanese macaques live on cold mountains in Japan. They sit in hot water pools to keep warm.

How smart are you?

We are very smart!

I use a stone to open the hard shell of a nut. Then I eat the nut inside.

Capuchin

Washing up

Macaque mums teach their young how to wash their food.

Q. How do you open a box of bananas?

A. Use a mon-key!

Clever chimps

Chimps are intelligent apes. They poke sticks into termite nests and use them to catch the tasty bugs.

13

Can you talk?

We can talk, but we don't use words.

We make lots of different sounds and pull lots of different faces.

Q. Why don't monkeys play cards in the jungle?

A. Because there are too many cheetahs!

Howler monkeys whoop and bark to each other

Angry ape
An adult male gorilla beats its chest with its hands when it is angry. It sounds like a drum.

Puzzle time

Can you solve all the puzzles?

Start here

Monkey maze

This monkey is so smart he found his way through the maze to find a banana. Are you as smart as him? Find your way to the middle of the maze.

Tell us apart

There are three differences between Mark and Matthew – can you spot them?

Mark

Matthew

Rhyme time

Only four of these words rhyme with 'ape'. Can you find them?

grape   mate   shape
scrape   bake   monkey
cape   chimp

True or false?

1. Monkeys and apes are primates.
2. Apes have tails.
3. Monkeys have hands with fingers and thumbs.

Monkey puzzle

Mother monkey climbed a tree and picked four bananas. Father monkey picked two plums. Baby monkey picked one mango. Can you work out how may pieces of fruit the monkey family had picked altogether?

Find the answers on page 25.

I am red, blue, gold, black, white and brown!

I am the most colourful of all primates.

Q. What did the monkey wear to cook dinner?

A. An ape-ron!

Mandrill

Good-looking
The De Brazza's monkey has a long white beard and an orange patch of fur above its eyes.

Big nose
Male proboscis monkeys have orange fur. Their noses are so big that they wobble when they run and jump.

Can your baby climb trees?

No, he is too young to climb trees.

My baby stays with me all of the time. He uses his hands to grab hold of my fur. I feed him with milk.

Squirrel monkeys

Lesson time

Monkeys teach their babies how to find food. They look under leaves for bugs, nuts and seeds.

Japanese macaques

Q. Why did the chimp go to the park?
A. To play on the monkey bars!

Young gorillas

Play time

Young monkeys and apes love to play. They climb trees and chase each other.

The Clever Monkey

Use your stickers to illustrate the story.

Once upon a time, there was an old man who earned his money by travelling around with a performing monkey. One evening the man came home looking sad and said, "The monkey is now too old to do his tricks. I will have to sell him to the butcher and make what money out of him I can."

The monkey heard this, and he decided to visit his friend the wild boar to ask him for help. The monkey sneaked out of the house and ran to the forest. He told the boar what his master had said. The boar

said, "Does your master have a baby?"

"Yes," said the monkey, "he has one son."

"Does it lie near the porch in the morning? I will come round early and take the baby and run off with it. Then you must run after me and rescue the baby. When the butcher comes they won't want to sell you."

The monkey thanked the boar and went home. The next day, everything happened as the boar had planned. The mother placed the baby near the porch while she tidied the house. Suddenly there was a noise in the porch and a cry from the baby. The mother called her husband, and they both ran to the porch door just in time to see the boar disappearing with their baby. Then they saw the

monkey running after
the thief.

The faithful monkey
brought the baby safely back to their arms.

"There!" said the wife. "This is the
animal you want to sell to the
butcher – if the monkey hadn't
been here we would have lost
our baby forever."

"You are right," said the man.
"You may send the butcher back when he comes."
And when the butcher arrived, he was sent
away. The monkey was well looked after
and lived the rest of his days in
peace and happiness.

Based on 'The Sagacious Monkey and the Boar'
by Yei Theodora Ozaki